EMMANUEL JOSEPH

The Balanced Visionary, Emotional Intelligence, Cultural Insight, and the Ethics of Innovation

Copyright © 2025 by Emmanuel Joseph

All rights reserved. No part of this publication may be reproduced, stored or transmitted in any form or by any means, electronic, mechanical, photocopying, recording, scanning, or otherwise without written permission from the publisher. It is illegal to copy this book, post it to a website, or distribute it by any other means without permission.

First edition

*This book was professionally typeset on Reedsy.
Find out more at reedsy.com*

Contents

1	Chapter 1: The Foundation of Emotional Intelligence	1
2	Chapter 2: Unveiling Cultural Insights	3
3	Chapter 3: The Ethics of Innovation	4
4	Chapter 4: Embracing Change	5
5	Chapter 5: Building Trust and Credibility	6
6	Chapter 6: The Role of Vision in Innovation	7
7	Chapter 7: Collaboration and Team Building	8
8	Chapter 8: Navigating Ethical Dilemmas	9
9	Chapter 9: Innovation and Social Responsibility	10
10	Chapter 10: Leadership and Emotional Intelligence	12
11	Chapter 11: Ethical Leadership	13
12	Chapter 12: The Power of Purpose	14
13	Chapter 13: Innovation and Cultural Diversity	15
14	Chapter 14: Balancing Innovation and Tradition	17
15	Chapter 15: The Future of Innovation	18

1

Chapter 1: The Foundation of Emotional Intelligence

Emotional intelligence (EI) forms the cornerstone of any balanced visionary's toolkit. It encapsulates the ability to perceive, interpret, and respond to not only one's own emotions but also the emotions of others. Understanding the depths of this concept begins with self-awareness. It is essential to identify personal emotional triggers and the resultant responses. This self-knowledge lays the groundwork for effective self-regulation, ensuring that reactions are proportionate and constructive.

However, EI is not solely introspective. Social awareness, a crucial aspect of EI, requires an acute sensitivity to the emotional states and needs of those around us. This awareness must be coupled with empathy, allowing the visionary to establish deep, meaningful connections. Empathy bridges the emotional gap, fostering an environment of mutual respect and understanding.

Beyond individual interactions, EI contributes to creating a cohesive, collaborative team environment. By understanding and managing team dynamics, a leader can cultivate a sense of belonging and collective purpose. EI paves the way for open communication, trust, and shared goals, which are the lifeblood of any innovative endeavor.

Ultimately, emotional intelligence is about leveraging emotions to facilitate thinking and problem-solving. It involves harnessing the power of emotions to drive motivation, resilience, and adaptability. A visionary with high EI is adept at navigating the complexities of human interactions, turning potential conflicts into opportunities for growth and collaboration.

2

Chapter 2: Unveiling Cultural Insights

In a world increasingly defined by global interactions, cultural insight is indispensable for any visionary. Understanding the diverse cultural landscapes within which we operate is crucial for fostering inclusive and innovative environments. Cultural intelligence begins with knowledge. This entails not only a familiarity with different cultural norms and practices but also an appreciation for the historical and social contexts that shape them.

However, knowledge alone is insufficient. It must be coupled with a genuine respect and curiosity for cultures different from one's own. This respect is demonstrated through actions that acknowledge and celebrate cultural diversity. Engaging with diverse perspectives enriches decision-making processes and inspires creativity by introducing a multitude of viewpoints.

Moreover, cultural insights facilitate effective communication across cultural boundaries. Misunderstandings and conflicts often arise from a lack of cultural awareness. By actively learning about and embracing cultural differences, a visionary can preemptively address potential areas of friction and foster a more harmonious work environment.

Cultural insight also plays a vital role in ethical decision-making. Recognizing the cultural dimensions of ethical dilemmas ensures that decisions are respectful and considerate of all stakeholders. It encourages a global perspective, reinforcing the importance of integrity and ethical standards in innovation.

3

Chapter 3: The Ethics of Innovation

Innovation, while a driver of progress and prosperity, carries with it profound ethical responsibilities. The ethical visionary is one who understands the broader implications of their innovations. This begins with a commitment to transparency and honesty. An innovator must be upfront about the potential impacts and limitations of their creations.

Ethical innovation also demands a proactive approach to addressing potential harms. This includes considering the environmental, social, and economic consequences of new technologies and processes. A balanced visionary weighs these factors carefully, striving to minimize negative impacts and maximize benefits for all stakeholders.

Furthermore, ethical innovation necessitates inclusivity. It is essential to involve diverse voices and perspectives in the innovation process. This ensures that the solutions developed are equitable and meet the needs of a broad spectrum of society. Inclusivity not only strengthens the ethical foundation of innovation but also enhances its relevance and effectiveness.

Lastly, the ethical visionary is committed to continuous learning and improvement. They remain vigilant to the evolving ethical landscape and are willing to adapt their practices accordingly. This ongoing commitment to ethical integrity reinforces trust and credibility, which are crucial for long-term success and societal impact.

4

Chapter 4: Embracing Change

Change is an inherent aspect of innovation. To be a balanced visionary, one must not only accept change but embrace it as a catalyst for growth. This begins with a mindset that views change as an opportunity rather than a threat. Such a mindset encourages curiosity and flexibility, key traits for navigating the ever-evolving landscape of innovation.

Adaptability is a crucial component of embracing change. It involves being open to new ideas and willing to pivot when necessary. This flexibility ensures that a visionary can respond to unforeseen challenges and leverage new opportunities. Adaptability also fosters a culture of continuous learning and improvement, vital for sustained innovation.

Moreover, embracing change requires resilience. The path of innovation is often fraught with setbacks and failures. A balanced visionary views these experiences as valuable learning opportunities. Resilience enables them to persevere through difficulties and maintain focus on their long-term vision.

Finally, embracing change involves fostering a culture that supports innovation. This includes encouraging experimentation, celebrating successes, and learning from failures. By creating an environment that nurtures creativity and risk-taking, a visionary can inspire their team to explore new possibilities and drive meaningful progress.

5

Chapter 5: Building Trust and Credibility

Trust and credibility are the bedrock of any successful endeavor. For a visionary, building and maintaining these qualities is paramount. Trust begins with integrity. This means being honest, transparent, and consistent in one's actions and decisions. Integrity fosters trust by demonstrating reliability and ethical behavior.

Credibility, on the other hand, is built through competence and expertise. A visionary must continually develop their skills and knowledge to stay at the forefront of their field. This ongoing commitment to excellence establishes credibility and reinforces trust.

Effective communication is also essential for building trust and credibility. Clear, honest, and open communication fosters understanding and transparency. It ensures that stakeholders are informed and engaged, creating a sense of shared purpose and collaboration.

Lastly, trust and credibility are reinforced through accountability. A visionary must take responsibility for their actions and decisions, acknowledging mistakes and learning from them. This accountability demonstrates a commitment to ethical behavior and continuous improvement, further strengthening trust and credibility.

6

Chapter 6: The Role of Vision in Innovation

A compelling vision is the driving force behind any innovative endeavor. It provides direction, purpose, and inspiration. For a visionary, crafting and articulating a clear, compelling vision is crucial. This vision serves as a guiding light, aligning the efforts of the team and ensuring that everyone is working towards a common goal.

A well-defined vision also fosters motivation and engagement. It provides a sense of purpose and meaning, inspiring individuals to give their best. By articulating a vision that resonates with their team, a visionary can cultivate a sense of ownership and commitment.

Moreover, a vision must be adaptable. The landscape of innovation is constantly changing, and a visionary must be willing to refine and evolve their vision in response to new challenges and opportunities. This adaptability ensures that the vision remains relevant and achievable.

Lastly, a vision must be communicated effectively. This involves not only sharing the vision but also demonstrating how it can be achieved. By providing a clear roadmap and tangible milestones, a visionary can inspire confidence and commitment, turning the vision into reality.

7

Chapter 7: Collaboration and Team Building

Collaboration is the heart of innovation. A balanced visionary understands that great ideas often come from diverse perspectives working together. Effective collaboration begins with building a diverse team. Diversity in skills, experiences, and backgrounds enriches the creative process and leads to more innovative solutions.

Creating a collaborative environment requires trust and open communication. Team members must feel safe to share their ideas and opinions without fear of judgment. A visionary fosters this environment by encouraging open dialogue, actively listening, and valuing each team member's contributions.

Furthermore, effective collaboration involves clear roles and responsibilities. By defining these roles, a visionary ensures that everyone understands their part in the collective effort. This clarity prevents misunderstandings and promotes efficiency, allowing the team to work seamlessly towards their common goals.

Lastly, collaboration extends beyond the immediate team. Building strong networks and partnerships with external stakeholders can provide valuable resources and insights. By leveraging these connections, a visionary can enhance their team's capabilities and drive greater innovation.

8

Chapter 8: Navigating Ethical Dilemmas

In the journey of innovation, ethical dilemmas are inevitable. A balanced visionary must navigate these challenges with integrity and sound judgment. Ethical decision-making begins with a clear understanding of one's values and principles. These values serve as a compass, guiding the visionary through complex ethical landscapes.

Transparency is crucial in addressing ethical dilemmas. Openly communicating the potential impacts and trade-offs of decisions helps build trust and credibility. It also ensures that stakeholders are informed and involved in the decision-making process, fostering a sense of shared responsibility.

Moreover, ethical decision-making requires a holistic perspective. A visionary must consider the broader implications of their actions, including social, environmental, and economic impacts. This comprehensive approach ensures that decisions are balanced and aligned with long-term goals.

Finally, a visionary must be willing to seek advice and collaborate with others when faced with ethical challenges. Consulting with diverse perspectives can provide valuable insights and help identify potential blind spots. This collaborative approach strengthens the ethical foundation of decision-making and promotes a culture of integrity.

9

Chapter 9: Innovation and Social Responsibility

Innovation is not just about creating new products or services; it's also about driving positive social change. A balanced visionary understands the importance of social responsibility and strives to create solutions that benefit society as a whole. This begins with a commitment to sustainability. Innovating in ways that minimize environmental impact and promote sustainable practices is essential for long-term success.

Social responsibility also involves addressing social inequalities. A visionary must strive to create inclusive solutions that empower marginalized communities and bridge social divides. This requires a deep understanding of social issues and a commitment to equity and justice.

Furthermore, social responsibility extends to the ethical use of technology. As technology continues to advance, it is crucial to consider the potential ethical implications and ensure that innovations are used responsibly. This includes safeguarding privacy, protecting against misuse, and promoting digital literacy.

Ultimately, social responsibility is about creating a positive impact. A visionary must align their innovation efforts with broader social goals, ensuring that their work contributes to the well-being of society. This commitment to social responsibility not only enhances the ethical foundation of innovation but also builds trust and credibility with stakeholders.

10

Chapter 10: Leadership and Emotional Intelligence

Leadership and emotional intelligence are deeply intertwined. A balanced visionary understands that effective leadership is not just about making decisions but also about inspiring and empowering others. Emotional intelligence enhances leadership by fostering a deep understanding of team dynamics and individual motivations.

An emotionally intelligent leader demonstrates empathy and compassion. They recognize and address the emotional needs of their team members, creating a supportive and inclusive work environment. This empathy builds trust and loyalty, motivating team members to give their best.

Moreover, emotional intelligence enhances conflict resolution. A visionary leader can navigate interpersonal conflicts with grace and fairness, ensuring that issues are resolved constructively. By addressing conflicts promptly and effectively, a leader fosters a harmonious and collaborative team environment.

Lastly, emotional intelligence in leadership involves self-awareness and self-regulation. A visionary leader is aware of their own emotions and how they impact their behavior. They can manage their emotional responses, ensuring that their actions align with their values and goals. This self-regulation enhances their credibility and effectiveness as a leader.

11

Chapter 11: Ethical Leadership

Ethical leadership is a cornerstone of a balanced visionary's approach. It involves leading with integrity, honesty, and a commitment to ethical principles. Ethical leaders set the tone for their organization, establishing a culture of trust and accountability.

An ethical leader prioritizes transparency. They communicate openly and honestly with their team, stakeholders, and the public. This transparency builds trust and ensures that everyone is informed and aligned with the organization's goals and values.

Moreover, ethical leadership involves making decisions that consider the broader impact on society and the environment. An ethical leader weighs the potential benefits and harms of their actions, striving to create positive outcomes for all stakeholders. This holistic approach ensures that the organization's success is sustainable and responsible.

Ethical leadership also requires courage. A visionary leader must be willing to stand up for their principles, even when faced with difficult decisions or opposition. This courage reinforces their commitment to ethical behavior and sets an example for others to follow.

12

Chapter 12: The Power of Purpose

Purpose is a powerful motivator for any visionary. It provides a sense of direction and meaning, guiding their efforts and decisions. A clear and compelling purpose inspires passion and commitment, driving innovation and progress.

A visionary with a strong sense of purpose can articulate their goals and vision with clarity and conviction. This clarity inspires others to join their mission, creating a sense of shared purpose and collective effort. By aligning their team's efforts with a common goal, a visionary can achieve greater impact and success.

Moreover, purpose-driven innovation is sustainable and resilient. A visionary who is guided by a clear purpose is more likely to persevere through challenges and setbacks. Their sense of purpose provides the motivation and determination needed to overcome obstacles and continue striving for their goals.

Ultimately, purpose is about making a positive impact. A balanced visionary is driven by a desire to create meaningful change and contribute to the well-being of society. This commitment to a higher purpose not only enhances the ethical foundation of their work but also inspires others to join their mission and make a difference.

13

Chapter 13: Innovation and Cultural Diversity

Cultural diversity is a powerful driver of innovation. A balanced visionary recognizes the value of diverse perspectives and actively seeks to incorporate them into their work. Embracing cultural diversity begins with creating an inclusive environment where all voices are heard and respected.

An inclusive environment fosters creativity and collaboration by bringing together different viewpoints and experiences. This diversity of thought leads to more innovative solutions and a deeper understanding of complex problems. By valuing and leveraging cultural diversity, a visionary can enhance the quality and impact of their work.

Moreover, cultural diversity promotes adaptability and resilience. Exposure to different cultures and ways of thinking broadens a visionary's perspective and enhances their ability to navigate change and uncertainty. This adaptability is crucial for staying relevant and competitive in a rapidly evolving world.

Ultimately, embracing cultural diversity is about recognizing and celebrating the richness of human experience. A balanced visionary understands that innovation thrives in an environment where diversity is not only accepted but actively sought and valued. This commitment to cultural diversity enhances the ethical foundation of innovation and promotes a more inclusive and equitable society.

14

Chapter 14: Balancing Innovation and Tradition

Innovation and tradition are often seen as opposing forces, but a balanced visionary understands the importance of integrating both. Tradition provides a foundation of stability and continuity, while innovation drives progress and change. Striking the right balance between these forces is crucial for sustainable success.

Tradition offers valuable insights and lessons from the past. By understanding and respecting these traditions, a visionary can build on the strengths of what has come before. This foundation provides a sense of identity and continuity, grounding innovation in a broader historical and cultural context.

Innovation, on the other hand, brings fresh perspectives and new possibilities. A visionary must be willing to challenge traditional boundaries and explore uncharted territory. This willingness to innovate ensures that their work remains relevant and responsive to changing needs and opportunities.

Balancing innovation and tradition involves a nuanced understanding of when to preserve and when to change. A visionary must carefully consider the potential impacts of their actions, ensuring that innovation enhances rather than undermines the positive aspects of tradition. This balanced approach promotes sustainable and meaningful progress.

15

Chapter 15: The Future of Innovation

The future of innovation holds immense promise and potential. As technology continues to advance and global challenges evolve, the role of the balanced visionary becomes increasingly important. A visionary must be forward-thinking, anticipating future trends and opportunities while remaining grounded in ethical principles.

Emerging technologies such as artificial intelligence, biotechnology, and renewable energy present exciting possibilities for the future. A visionary must stay informed about these developments and explore how they can be harnessed for positive impact. This forward-thinking approach ensures that their work remains relevant and impactful.

Moreover, the future of innovation requires a commitment to sustainability and social responsibility. As global challenges such as climate change and social inequality intensify, a visionary must prioritize solutions that promote long-term well-being and equity. This commitment to ethical and responsible innovation is crucial for addressing the complex issues of the future.

Ultimately, the future of innovation is shaped by the visionaries who lead it. By embodying the principles of emotional intelligence, cultural insight, and ethical integrity, a balanced visionary can drive meaningful progress and create a better future for all.

Book Description: The Balanced Visionary: Emotional Intelligence, Cultural Insight, and the Ethics of Innovation

CHAPTER 15: THE FUTURE OF INNOVATION

In a world defined by rapid change and global interconnectedness, "The Balanced Visionary: Emotional Intelligence, Cultural Insight, and the Ethics of Innovation" explores the essential qualities of a true visionary leader. This thought-provoking book delves into the critical role of emotional intelligence in understanding and managing human emotions, the importance of cultural insight in fostering inclusivity and creativity, and the ethical responsibilities that come with driving innovation.

Through a series of insightful chapters, readers will discover how to navigate the complexities of human interactions, embrace diverse perspectives, and balance the forces of tradition and change. With a focus on sustainable and responsible innovation, this book provides a comprehensive guide for leaders seeking to make a positive impact in their organizations and society.

Filled with practical wisdom and real-world examples, "The Balanced Visionary" offers a roadmap for developing the skills and mindset needed to thrive in an ever-evolving landscape. Whether you are a seasoned leader or an aspiring innovator, this book will inspire and equip you to lead with integrity, empathy, and vision.

www.ingramcontent.com/pod-product-compliance
Lightning Source LLC
LaVergne TN
LVHW020509080526
838202LV00057B/6264